Return to Yesterplace

Copyright © 2021 by Susan Lindsley, all rights reserved. No portion of this book may be reproduced, stored or transmitted in any form or by any means without written permission from Susan Lindsley and/or ThomasMax Publishing. An exception is granted for brief excerpts taken for review purposes.

ISBN-13: 978-1-7377620-2-7

ISBN-10: 1-7377620-2-1

First printing, October 2021

Published by:

ThomasMax Publishing
P.O. Box 250054
Atlanta, GA 30325

Return to Yesterplace

Susan Lindsley

ThomasMax
Your Publisher
For The 21st Century

Praise for Return to Yesterplace

Susan Lindsley's latest collection is a hybrid of photos and poetry, each complementing the other in exploring themes related to nature and to the human condition. The works have nuances of pastoral influences, but the exception here is the authenticity of the poet in rendering experiences with places and creatures she knew firsthand. This isn't the case of a city poet glorifying nature from a distance—it's a work depicting a deep kinship with the culture and landscape of her youth.

The book would be a pleasing means of sharing poems with family and friends, readily accessible and avoiding much of the obscurity characterizing contemporary poetry. Reading the work is like listening to a babbling brook, and it sends the reader alongside the poet on a journey into times present and, in the author's own words, "Yesterplace; Home of the Heart."
-- Kay B. Day/author and columnist

I love the Southern music, the rock and roll, the love-song lyrical power of Susan Lindsley's poems. Like the moon makes waves at its own time and pace, Susan's poems remind us how we live our own adventures of love and loss and living in the South. Her poems jog our memories as time pushes against the small of our backs, saying take us with you, take us with you! Her poems take me back and sometimes going back is all I want to do. Every award she gets is a testament to her excellent writing!
-- Peggy June Mercer BMI Georgia Author of the Year, 2011

What the world needs now is more books like Susan Lindsley's *Return to Yesterplace*. So many of us have taken to the woods now and again, seeking the solace of nature's constancy as we've fought our way through a changed world. We've felt our burden of change and dread melt away with each step into a wooded place or a park, and we've come back to our responsibilities eased a bit, feeling settled and stronger. That's what it's like to journey into Lindsley's "Yesterplace." Each poem, each photo, quiets us in a strengthening way, and we are mighty glad that we could go away to the place she has given us, just to come home again believing in the possibility of a kinder world.
-- Dana Wildsmith, author, *One Light*

ACKNOWLEDGMENTS

The picture of the train in downtown Milledgeville was provided by Randy Ellis and taken by Eugene Ellis. Thank you, Randy. Our town was known nationwide as the only town in the United States where a train had to stop for a traffic light.

Frank Herring painted the watercolor of Westover on the cover, which shows the house as it was in 1930. The original hangs in the home of Lillas Lindsley James.

Special thanks also to the three poets who reviewed my manuscript and commented for the reader. Dana, Peggy and Kay have supported me and my work since I was one of their students at a Southeastern Writers Workshop.

Special thanks to my publisher, Lee Clevenger, for tackling this complex project and producing a beautiful book for me.

For Gail

*Thanks for the best twenty-five years
anyone could hope for*

OTHER BOOKS BY SUSAN LINDSLEY

Novels, Southern historical
    The Bottom Rail
    When Darkness Fell

Memoirs
    Blue Jeans and Pantaloons in YESTERPLACE
    Possum Cops, Poachers and the Counterfeit Game Warden

Biography
    Susan Myrick of Gone With the Wind
    The Lindsleys of Westover

Collections of others' works edited
    Myrick Memories: From Plantation to Town (1900-1950s)
    Margaret Michell: A Scarlett or a Melanie? (Susan Myrick essays)
    Luther Lindsley: His Literary Works

Poetry
    O Yesterplace and other poems (out of print)
    Christmas Gift
    When Yestertime Was Now
    Whisper of Love

Short Story collections
    Emperor of the United American States
    Whitetails and Tall Tales
    Finding Bigfoot
    Tales Over Time

Specialty books
    Wildlife in Persimmon Paradise (photography)
    Whitetail Secrets (photography, coming soon)

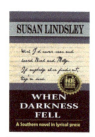
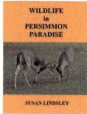
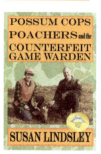

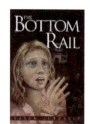

KUDZU

Kudzu climbs upon the pine,
Kudzu,
Reaching,
Grasping,
Clinging vine.

Deep beneath the sod it roots
Reaching out ten thousand shoots.

Like a shroud or warm embrace
Hugging trees until no trace
Of anything is left to see—
Not a pine or maple tree—
Just the rising clinging vine,
Ever growing kudzu vine.

YESTERPLACE
Home of the Heart

Rolling hills and meadows
Spreading country smells into the air.

Long forgotten daffodils
Blooming by a home's remains.

Wooden rocking chairs
Squeaking on a shady porch.

Azaleas and crepe myrtle
Scenting country air.

Dragon flies and honey bees
Buzzing shaded streams.

Beaver pond below the spring
Doubling daffodils.

Diamonds of the morning mist
Gleaming spider webs.

Bacon crisp as peanut brittle
Scenting morning air.

Twilight lines of cattle
Lowing homeward down the hill.

Ducks in misty dawn
Cracking mirrors of the lakes.

Roosters in the morning twilight
Crowing day awake.

Blueticks and a redbone
Barking treed in early night.

Memories like tsunamis
Echoing Yesterplace.

Grandmother Thulia Kate Myrick, Aunt Katie Myrick Lowerre, and Aunt Susan Myrick (consultant to *Gone With the Wind*) take to the rocking chairs in the shade.

MILLEDGEVILLE

How well do I remember all those days of long ago
When Trigger and Roy Rogers played the local picture show,

The times that *Post* and *Collier's* came each week by R. F. D.
And Jessie's "Golden Slipper" was the only play to see.

When wagons filled the alleys and the train ran down the street
And every horse had horseshoes but the children had bare feet.

A place we all had gardens but we had no telephone
And doors were always open although everyone was gone.

When the horses ran away the night the Pageant played
The tale of history of our town two hours was delayed.

I still remember WAVES who marched across the college square,
And soldiers finding welcome here—in war we used to care.

Oh, Milledgeville is home today as it was home back then,
For every time I go away, I just come home again.

TREASURES

I have seen the sun rise to a morning crimson red
And seen the twilight turn to gold a rising thunderhead.

I have seen the mountains when the mist was hanging low
And seen the summer Rockies with a running ridge of snow.

I have seen the deserts come to life with sudden showers
And seen a thousand valleys turned to rainbows by the flowers.

Oh, I have seen the treasures of the lowlands and the hills,
But Beauty stores her treasures in the golden daffodils.

BEYOND FOREVER

We have been together since before I can remember,
Long before the leaves were ever gilded in September.

We were loving long before there ever was a spring,
Before the stars were shining or the nightingale could sing.

We were holding hands together, standing side by side,
A thousand years before the moon had ever pulled the tide.

We were lovers long ago, before the birds could fly,
Long before a rainbow ever crossed a summer sky.

Since before there was a time, I know we've been together,
And together we shall be somewhere beyond forever.

THE CHAPEL

I found a tiny chapel hidden deep within a wood
And started to go in—but wondered if I should.

Indecisive, standing there, I turned to walk away
But halted at the sharp command that ordered me to "Stay!"

"Come in, come in, and look around! Don't keep on standing there,
For you are now on holy ground, a land for peace and prayer."

I looked ahead and then behind but no one could I see,
For no one else was anywhere. Had I been hearing me?

I stepped inside the chapel but the floor was only ground
And like a million rainbows there were flowers all around.

I knelt there in the chapel and I bowed my head to pray
And knew that I was home again, home again to stay

For then I looked to heaven, where the ceiling was the sky,
The chapel was within my heart—I used to pass it by.

TWILIGHT

Twilight—
    And the bell is tolling vespers
    From the church that sits alone
    Upon the hill...

Twilight—
    And the silent mist is rising
    Over darkening waters of the pool
    Beside the mill....

Twilight—
    And the falling sun
    Is turning all the clouds
    To streams...

Twilight—
    And the gentle hand of Darkness
    Spreads her softest blanket
    For my dreams.

LILLIAN

Dawning
And the tumbling maple leaves
Decorate the morning
Like a summer shower
Filled with scarlet and with gold.

How many years have gone
Since you and I saw morning
Side by side
Beneath the maple trees
And waded in the waters of the lake
Into the chilly waters of Winnipesaukee—
And filled the autumn air
With laughter
Rich and scarlet as the autumn leaves?

So young we were
And oh, so much we loved in youth.
We knew no sorrow then
And never thought of fear
Or death
And never dreamed of separation
Soon to come,
So many years ago.
But as the maple leaves began to fall
I found you once again
And wrote
The many words we never spoke
Those many years ago.
But with the morning post
The letter came,
Unopened,
With but a single word beside your name
"Deceased."

THE WEST WIND

The west wind blows
A dusty dry aroma
From the fields of hay,
And I remember you
And summer
And the sea...

The west wind blows
A touch of frost
From winter far away,
And I remember you
And autumn
And the golden maple leaves...

The west wind blows
A heavy sudden storm
And fields of pristine snow,
And I remember you
And winter walks
And cider steaming by the open fire...

The west wind blows
The sweet quick scent of spring
And music far away,
And I remember you
And love
And yesterday
And Oh! what sweet tomorrows
Still to come.

THE ROOSTER

Long before the sun awoke, I heard a rooster crow,
Returning me to yesterplace and all I used to know,

To the days of childhood and the country home I knew,
To the land of reddish dirt where corn and cotton grew,

To the days of racing rain to gather in the hay
When every day in summer was a watermelon day,

To the days of swimming in the pond down by the mill
And riding favorite horses over meadows and the hill,

To the days of waiting for the bus in winter cold,
And crossing one-way bridges even then so quaint and old,

To the frosty mornings that were lacy fairy lands,
Melting frost on windows with my naked, freezing hands,

To the warmth and comfort of an evening by the fire,
And Sundays when the preachers preached another kind of fire.

To the days of splendor and of youth so long ago—
Perhaps again tomorrow I will hear that rooster crow.

ONE THOUSAND YEARS

I wonder if I walked upon this earth a thousand years ago
Did I live within a valley where the beaver rivers flow?

Did I see the otter sliding to the river in a rush?
Or know a thousand years ago the music of the mockingbird and thrush?

Did I walk into the mountains where the elk in summer graze
And was it there a thousand years ago I grew to love the morning haze?

A thousand years ago did I walk in silence over fallen autumn leaves
But today I dance with them inside my soul because of all the colors spread about by
  autumn freeze?

Did I wander over prairies where I sought the speedy bouncing deer?
A thousand years ago did people hunt each other or was going hungry then the only thing we had to fear?

Did I welcome springtime then with all the joy and wonder springtime brings today
When I see the dogwoods and the daffodils and all the rainbow colors that will always come in May?

Or did I live a thousand years ago beside the sea
So even then the pulse that beats within the ocean beat in me?

Or is the land where now I tread the very sod I walked upon a thousand years ago
Where chestnuts are a memory on the land where now the oak and hickory grow?

But concrete covers meadows now, and all the trails I might have walked a thousand years ago
Are covered now in asphalt; and in another thousand years no one will even know
The song of warblers or the sound of pines in summer breeze;
Flowers will no longer riot across the meadows
And hickory won't be growing here to cover all the land with golden leaves.

Everywhere the deer and turkey trod will be but miles of granite markers where the human bodies lie,
And power lines will eat their way across the land and fill up all the air where once, so long ago, the birds could fly.
The world will be a parking lot and windmills rising tall into the sky,
And in a thousand years will there even breathe a human soul to wonder why?

GEORGIA II

Have you seen the sunlight on a hyacinth in the snow
Or walked upon the mountains where the wild azaleas grow?

Have you seen the morning clouds hugging mountain sides
Or felt the sands beneath your feet go running with the tides?

Have you seen the autumn rain of red and golden leaves
Or seen the earth uplifted by a frosty winter freeze?

Have you seen the lightning standing tall against the sky
Or have you heard the calling geese when they were flying by?

Have you heard the music of the quail on summer days
Or seen the wind caress the grass to make it flow in different ways?

Oh, memories of my youthful years are better now than then
So home I'll go to Georgia where I'll live them once again.

MY LOVE

I met you somewhere long ago,
Far off across the sea,
And somewhere in the desert sands
You whispered love to me.

Somewhere in the long ago,
A thousand years away,
You loved me in the moonlight
Where the knights and dragons stay.

When the gods were walking
On the earth so long ago
They discovered we found a love
Beyond the love they know.

The love that came from yesterday,
Before there was a star,
Will be with us tomorrow still
No matter where we are.

WE MATTER NOT ...

The things I have touched and owned so long,
This Marlin I have carried to the woods for all these years now gone,
Whose hands will hold it in the years that lie ahead
And take it to the woods when I am dead?

The fighting stallions I so love, the rearing steeds
Standing on the mantle, will another ever heed
Their silent call and give them both the special space
Within a home, displaying all their beauty and their grace,
Caressing them each day as I have done
Until the lamplight on their coat is like the sun
Upon a thoroughbred—
Who will love my stallions when I'm dead?

All these many books I love so well
Because of all the wonders and adventures that they tell
In poetry and in prose—
Stories of the cowboys and of horses and of farmers planting rows
Of corn across the plains
And facing hordes of locusts or unending days of bleakness and of rains,
The legends of the heroes living in the long ago
And all the poems of beauty and of love—will they all go
Into the dump, these books I long have read,
And all the magic they hold for me be lost forever when I'm dead?

Who will get the pictures when I'm gone,
Pictures of the trips I've been on
And taken with such love and care
And put them into books and labeled where
I was and all the birds I saw, and places too—
The mountains stark and grey against the blue,
The rocky ocean shore
And sands going on until the eye can see no more—
Who will want the picture of the rainbow and the summer thunderhead,
The courting whitetails and the elk,
And my thousand other pictures when I'm dead?
All the words I write, of love and pain,
Of sunshine and of rain,
Of sheep that speckle white the Scottish hills,
And, favorite of them all, my daffodils—

Will all this music of my heart and soul be read,
Or will they throw away the lines I write as soon as I am dead?
Who will love this land of pine and oak where deer and turkey through the shadows go?
Who will tend the land and plant the seed and help persimmons grow?
All are oh so eager for the land of softly rolling meadows and the timber-shaded hills
And all would be so happy for the pond where every year I've added just a few more daffodils.

Who will hold the land I love as dear as is to me
When all the land around is growing homes, and dollars marching on the land is all the others see?

Will someone ever care enough to walk where raccoons tread
And gather up persimmon seeds and plant them on the land I love when I am dead?

Or will old Yellowstone explode at last
And turn our windmills and the concrete into our unremembered past?

For in the scheme of time and tide, we matter not a jot
And all we are and what we love are very soon forgot.

DECATUR CIVIC CHORUS

I hear the crystal music floating in the evening air
Like a silver butterfly or softly whispered prayer,

I hear the drumming like the tramping of the feet
Of a mighty army marching to a martial beat,

Silver notes come trilling like a whisper on the breeze
Caressing every syllable like wind upon the leaves.

The voices like the daffodils that dance beside the stream,
Are rich as all the lollipops in every childhood dream.

Music flows like rivers spreading over valleys wide
And rises in crescendo like the mighty ocean tide.

A waterfall cascading, it is rippling through the night
With every note a dewdrop catching early morning light,

Like the sunset colors or the wisdom of the old
The music fills the hollows of the hungry, empty soul.

Forever, like my heartbeat, will the music sing to me—
It's in my soul for always, like a sacred memory.

MY FLAG

I saw a cardinal sitting on the snow against the sky;
The colors took me to a time my flag was passing by,

Memories brought an echo of the drumming and the beat,
The blaring of the bugle and the tramp of marching feet,

The blast of firing volleys and the final bugle call,
Reminders of the soldiers who have given us their all.

How well did I remember years of service to my land
And what a thrill it was to lead my troops behind the band.

I watched the red bird spread his wings and lift into the sky,
And snapped to full attention, for my flag was passing by.

THE DOOLEY CAT

The Dooley Cat
So fair
Sat
Upon the chair
And made a place
To sleep
Upon the face
Of a sheep
On the cushion there,
 And her hair
Turned it white
Overnight.
And if you sit upon the chair
Where Dooley sat,
Why then
You'll have the hair
Of the cat
Where you sat
And you won't sit there
Again.

NOVEMBER

The golden aura of the early morning
Chases silent dawn with silent breeze
While lifting over distant hills the sun
Turns away an early autumn freeze.

Spiders spinning webbing through the night
Hang their diamond dresses out to dry;
A whippoorwill calls softly to the dawning
And flings a note of joy into his cry;

Crafty Winter scampers quickly into morning,
Ever hoping lingering Summer he will meet;
Gleeful Autumn hurries Summer into history
And spreads a golden carpet for her feet.

SEASONS

I
Love
Autumn,
Thanksgiving,
Holidays from school,
Flights of honking geese,
Bunnies, fox and deer at twilight
Slipping in blue shadows for persimmons.

I
Love
Winter,
Snowfalls
And Georgia mud
That rises on the frost
And crunches under foot
When I walk across the barnyard.

I
Love
Spring
Chasing winter
And bringing me
Days of daffodils and
Violets, and azaleas throwing
Shadows over lilies white and green.

I
Love
Summer
And July sun,
Swimming holes
Where tadpoles and
The minnows swim and
Bullfrogs croak and bellow.

If I
Must
Choose
A season
And a place
For me upon the
The earth to never leave,
I must select the springtime
And my yesterplace, where in
My heart I frolic with the fawns
And waltz across the greening fields
To music of the stars and moonlit breeze.

OLD OCONEE RIVER

Where cattle softly sounding close of day
Meander in the twilight in the field,
Where all the smells of Christmas linger on
With fragrance of the cedar on the hill,

Where winter always welcomes early spring
And summer welcomes every newborn fawn,
Where trumpet vine and jasmine waltz together
And life begins anew with every dawn,

Where passing clouds are pictures in the heavens
And winter-weary trees applaud the breeze,
Where yellow bells are smiling with the morning
And ice lifts up the earth with every freeze,

Where blossoms cover green with bridal white
And flowers fill the air with sweet perfumes,
Where meadow larks are singing every morning
And every spring the crimson clover blooms.

Where morning mist drapes diamonds on the trees
And winter sky is sun and cobalt blue,
Where every springtime shower brings a rainbow
And every dream I dream can still come true,

Where dawn finds not a ripple on the river
And trees gaze in the gliding looking glass,
Where beaver and the otter live together
And red-wings dance upon the Johnson grass,

Where dogwoods dress like virgins every spring

And flowers every season line the street,
Where people dream of springtime all the winter
And every day our youth and history meet,

Where bluebirds chase the sunlight every morning
And meadows smell of hay or smell of loam,
Where daffodils are dancing without reason,
The old Oconee River calls me home.

I'LL THINK OF YOU...

When I walk alone along the coast
I'll think of you.

I'll think of you beneath the robes of grey,
The silent, weeping moss
That sweeps beneath the oaks.

I'll think of you by waterfalls weeping misty tears into the air,
And every time I see a mountain valley turning through the smoky hills,
I'll think of you.

Each uniform I see I'll think of you,
And I'll remember tears I could not weep
While crying in my soul
When I heard Taps at twilight.

I'll think of you when whippoorwills
Call to seek a lover in the dark and empty night,
Or when a deer slips into a meadow in the early morning mists
I'll think of you.

Each lake or pond or river that I see
I'll think of you
And hear your laughter lifting with the bass that rise to bait.
You are all around me in my life so no matter where I go,
I'll think of you.

When I see foxes play
Or jonquils toss their yellow heads and dance beneath the sun
Or violets blush in shadows under pines,
I'll think of you.

When I see our flag unfurled
Or hear the songs we both went marching by,
I'll think of you.
But when the bugle sounds,
A volley's fired,
Or Taps is played,
I'll weep for missing you.

THE NIGHT WIND

Like a whisper far away the night wind calls to me
And speaks to me of love that was or maybe is to be,

I feel her lover's arms and the warmth of her embrace,
Oh so gently does the night wind touch her kisses to my face.

The lyrics that she sings tonight are songs that lovers sing,
Of golden skies at twilight and of flowers and of spring.

She brings me many gifts and she never makes demands,
Oh, what sweet perfumes she brings from many distant lands.

Like a smitten lover the night wind stirs the trees
To gather me a garland and to shower me leaves.

So while the moon is hanging like a lantern in the sky
We dance across the meadows through the night, the wind and I.

THE PENOBSCOT RIVER

Younger than tomorrow and yet older than the tide,
O Mighty River, tell me of your secrets deep inside:

Do the otters swim with you and dance upon your shore?
In the sky above you do the hawk and eagle soar?

Did the glaciers give you birth upon some distant hill
Or springs that rose among the rocks to feed a mountain rill?

Do you crash in mighty falls from on the mountain high,
Throwing foam and mist upon the wind and to the sky?

In a valley far away, a valley green and lush,
Do you house a beaver pond with lilies and with rush?

Do you water farmers' fields while on your seaward run
Or make a favorite swimming hole with oak and rope and sun?

You're ever so reflective in the sun and moonlight streams
And bring the rainbow colors ever night into my dreams.

Will these deep reflections be forever mine to keep
Or will the otter laugh at me each night when I'm asleep?

When you reach the ocean and you become the tide
Will you forget the mountains where the hawk and eagle cried?

WHEN I WAS VERY YOUNG

When I was very young and ran so free,
My neighbors down the dusty country road would take their hounds into the night, and take me
To listen to their music as they followed on a raccoon's trail wherever it would lead;
We'd follow through the night as soon as sounds of baying said they'd treed
A possum or a coon.

On some early autumn frosty nights we had a moon
So bright
We didn't even need the light
That flowed like golden water from the lanterns on the leaves.

Those were days when shoes were foreign to my feet until the hardest winter freeze
Would lift the barnyard dirt like icing on a homemade chocolate layer cake,
And when I walked across the naked frozen ground I loved to hear the tinkling that the falling shards would make.

Even then I loved the land where Cherokee and Creek so many years ago
Had made a home and left me arrowheads to find in every hollow where the springs begin to
  flow,
And how I loved to hunt them when a child—and still today—these relics made of stone
That set imagination free to make those distant yesterdays my very own.

How I loved the streams and all the crawfish there, and all the tadpoles too—
I would catch and put them into a bowl and watch until they grew
Their legs and lost their tails and then I'd set them free.

Much fun for me
Was a Georgia puffing adder in a box so everyone could see
His funny snout
And take the time to watch him playing dead and learn that snakes are not about
The fall of Adam and the birth of sin,
But rather they are creatures filled with beauty if you have an open mind to let the beauty in.

The greatest fun was riding over hills, and teaching tricks I'd seen in movies to my horse.
I tried to teach her everything that Trigger did, of course.

But now I walk across the land with shoes upon my feet
And on my wanderings when I find a stump or fallen log, I take a seat
To let my weary bones have just a momentary rest
While thinking back to long ago, for now that I am growing old, it seems remembering
    is the one thing I do best.

SILVER

I was ten
Barefooted,
Country.
She was old
Dabbled gray
Unhitched
From the plow
For noontime break.

I turned a bucket
Upside down
At her left side
For a stepping stone,
Crawled onto her back,
Wrapped my left fist in her mane,
Raised my right hand
And yelled,
"Hi ho, Silver!
Away!"

THE SEA

Sighing like a lover longing for the lost Lenore,
Sounding, ever sounding, pounding rocks along the shore,

Softly like a whisper, like a whisper while asleep,
Silent as the promise of the secrets she will keep,

Silver in the morning mist, silver, soft and white,
Till the burning sun has turned the ocean burning bright,

Black as Satan's temper when the sea is tempest tossed,
Going into mourning when another life is lost,

Breathing, ever breathing, like a soft and gentle sigh,
Breathing, ever heaving like a giant about to die,

Changing, ever changing, like a naughty willful child,
Meek in early morning, in the evening free and wild,

Changing, ever changing with the sun and wind and tide—
For never on the rolling sea can constancy abide.

MEMORIES

Memories walk the sands I've walked along the ocean side,
Flowing like the sands forever molded by the tide.

Memories whisper like the sound of footsteps on the trail
Winding through the mountains where I heard the panther wail.

Memories burst with color like the flowers of the spring,
Making me nostalgic with the music memories sing.

Memories flicker softly like a distant candle light,
Beacons of tomorrow like the Milky Way at night.

Memories like the mountain mist are curling through my soul
Making yesterday today as I am growing old.

VISIONS AT SYMPHONY

Yellow kites on morning breeze,
Moonlight glow on summer seas.
Children laughing at their play,
Lighthouse, flashing by the bay.
Sailing ships that catch the tide,
Rivers where the otters slide.
Autumn scarlet in the skies,
Morning mist that starts to rise,
Redtails soaring over hills,
Winter snow on daffodils.
Sunlight on a shadowed stream,
Flying clouds of whipping cream,
Waterfalls and rainbow mist,
Cactus that the snow has kissed.
Snowfall on a cedar tree—
Pictures in a symphony.

CAPE BRETON

Solitude and ocean walks, and eagles flying free,
Spruce and hemlock on the hills and thunder from the sea,

Darkness in the midnight sky, untouched by human light,
A million billion stars that make the midnight darkness bright,

Whispers in the evening from the rising autumn breeze,
Dancing rainbow colors in the birch and maple leaves,

Rivers rising on the hills and foaming for the sea,
Making polished marble from the falling, rolling scree,

Kisses in the ocean winds that mist the distant hill,
Dreams of peace and solitude Cape Breton can fulfill.

DREAMS OF YESTERPLACE

I heard the rooster crowing in the frigid winter air,
Calling like an echo buried in the soul somewhere,
Calling up the memories of the dawns so long ago—
Summers of the peafowl and the winter's silent snow,

Dawning when the cattle feasted quietly on the lawn
Chewing up the flowers ere the rooster crowed at dawn,

Mornings when the very earth was lifted up on ice
That fell beneath my footsteps like some dominoes or dice,

Mornings in the summer when the air was hot and dry
And pagan dances only left a hot and cloudless sky,

Mornings when the winter lost its grip upon the hills
To the white of dogwoods and the gold of daffodils.

On this winter dawn when all the trees are naked lace
I decorate the morning with my dreams of yesterplace.

REMEMBERING TWENTY-FIVE YEARS

What joy you brought to life,
Each day a new adventure.
We had days of dogs and cats
Autumn hikes across the woods
Among the crimson and the gold.

We strolled the beach together,
Dodging wavelets and the gulls
Forever seeking visions
Of the eagle or the osprey.

We hiked on mountain trails
With bells upon our feet
To warn the bears
*We come into your world
And hope to leave alive.*

We heard the bugling elk,
Saw the whitetails
And the black tail deer,
The muleys
And the tiny ones down in the Keys.

We watched the gobblers strut,
Saw Rocky Mountain goats and sheep,
And shared a hilltop with a moose in Nova Scotia.

We shivered in the snow
And relished desert sun,
Saw cactus capped with snow,
Listened to coyotes wailing out their lonely
And shared a lunchtime with a bobwhite quail.

We flew to foreign lands,
Saw castles, bunnies,
And the fallow deer
And walked the castle halls
Where my family lives today
Since a thousand years ago.

On a rocky cliff in Nova Scotia
Cape Breton winds
Collapsed our tent at midnight
And almost blew us both into the sea.

In the Southland
When a storm became a funnel
We once again escaped a fatal fate.

We watched the autumn chills
Flame our mountains
With colors bright enough to make us blink.

We travelled to the swamps and bayous
Where me meet the rattler and the gator
And far too many birds to ever count.

At spring training for the Braves and Sox
We trilled to watch the pitching
Of both Lester and of Shilling
And to talk for just a moment with the Yaz.

We saw the magic of the warped,
Grotesque and dead
Turned to beauty in the wood,
Artwork by the wind and sea,
Or by the hand of God.

We walked the sacred soil
Of battlefields
Where dreams and soldiers died
And our nation rose and almost fell.

Return to Yesterplace

Now Covid keeps us home
But also keeps our dreams alive
To venture once again on endless journeys
To the woods, the hills and sea,
To watch the autumn blaze the mountains,
To feel once more the tide pull sand from under foot
And share whatever pathways we might find.

What joys you brought to me
And will bring on all tomorrows,
From the mountains, sea and marshes
Still to share.

FACING OUR WINTER

Let's sit together on the porch and watch the bluebirds fly
And hand-in-hand go strolling while a rainbow paints the sky.

Let's sit together in the swing and hear the whippoorwills
And in the early spring let's pick a thousand daffodils.

Let's listen for the gobbling from the pines up on the hill
And snuggle by the fire to ward off early autumn chill.

Let's wander deep into the woods where wild azaleas grow
And stroll together down the trails where deer and bunnies go.

Winter lies so close ahead, our autumn now is gone,
So let us live and love and laugh while we are flesh and bone.

WHEN I AM DEAD

When I am dead
And what I was is scattered
In the daffodils,
I will no longer smell the coffee
In the morning
Or hear the bobwhite
Calling to his mate.

I will not feel the sunlight
Or turn my face to welcome falling snow.
The kitten's purr will only hum in silence
And I will not feel her flex her paws in joy
Upon my chest.
I will no longer hear the hounds
Pursing possums or raccoons
And barking their delight
As they run across the ground
Where I am lying.

If I can never smell magnolias
Or the lilies
Or hear the music of the mockingbird
Or hoofbeats of the whitetails running by,
But still the human soul
Should live forever,
I pray whatever gods may be
To let mine stay
Where I have lived,
To roam the woods,
The meadows
And the streams,
To ride the mustangs,
Sail the winds,
And waltz with butterflies
On rainbows
To the songs of meadowlarks.

CPSIA information can be obtained
at www.ICGtesting.com
Printed in the USA
LVHW070609070422
715541LV00006B/128